DayOne

HELP!

I FEEL ASHAMED

Sue Nicewander

Consulting Editor: Dr. Paul Tautges

© Day One Publications 2012

First printed 2012

ISBN 978-1-84625-320-1

Scripture quotations, unless stated otherwise, are
from the New King James Version. Copyright © 1982
by Thomas Nelson, Inc.

Published by Day One Publications
Ryelands Road, Leominster, HR6 8NZ

TEL 01568 613 740 FAX 01568 611 473

email—sales@dayone.co.uk

UK web site—www.dayone.co.uk

USA web site—www.dayonebookstore.com

All rights reserved

No part of this publication may be reproduced, or stored in a
retrieval system, or transmitted, in any form or by any means,
mechanical, electronic, photocopying, recording or otherwise,
without the prior permission of Day One Publications.

Designed by **documen**
Printed by Orchard Press Cheltenham Ltd

Contents

Shannon's[1] uncle sexually abused her throughout her childhood. He told her that she was a seductress and that she would be punished if she told anyone. Ashamed, Shannon was silent for years. As she grew older her uncle's cruel ridicule and humiliation crushed her spirit.

Shannon's parents were unaware of the abuse. At one point Shannon tried to tell her mother, who expressed shock and disbelief. She reprimanded Shannon for telling lies that could destroy her uncle's reputation. Nothing was done to protect her, so the abuse continued.

Though Shannon had received the Lord Jesus Christ as her Savior when she was a young child, her mother's reaction shook Shannon's faith in God and caused her to doubt her family's love. During

[1] Shannon and Gwen are fictional characters created from
     true stories, with some details changed to protect identities.

her teen years, her anger grew into a bitterness and rebellion that were met with condemnation and sharp criticism from her family. Shannon withered and hardened under their disapproval. She married young to escape her home and her uncle, not realizing that her new husband was as troubled as she was. They divorced after a few months, intensifying her family's disapproval. Shannon sought emotional relief by plunging into self-destructive partying and immorality. But nothing satisfied the ache in her soul.

Some years later, Shannon was experiencing panic attacks, failed relationships, angry outbursts, and depression that sometimes required hospitalization. Eventually she remembered her abandoned faith in Christ and decided that it was time for a change: time to return to the Lord.

She joined a doctrinally sound Christ-centered church and there sought counseling to overcome her anger, depression, and fear. The gospel became fresh again as she started to understand that the love and presence of God had protected her soul. She received his forgiveness and learned to trust God more and more. Her uncle had died, but Shannon forgave her mother and asked her parents to forgive her. Gradually her relationship with them began to mend.

Today, Shannon's new church continues to provide her with help through Bible-based teaching, biblical love, godly fellowship, prayer support, and practical living skills. She holds a job with a Christian business-owner and has returned to college. She's now ready to move on with her life.

Shannon's Private Struggle

Shannon knows that she is on the right track now. She experiences periods of peace and enjoyment. Her new friendships are healthy and growing. But she still feels ashamed of her past. Her friends do not know about the abuse or her rebellion, and Shannon fears discovery. "What would they think? How could they want to befriend an awful person like me?"

Doubts cloud her mind. Her fears lead her to analyze every conversation. She mentally flogs people for their insensitivities or degrades herself for her social blunders. Surely people are angry with her! Are they secretly whispering behind her back? Will they turn away, like everyone else? Or, worse, will they turn on her? She cringes and bristles at the thought.

At times her inner battle becomes very intense. When dark thoughts and doubts persist, her confusion and burden grow heavier, and she wants to withdraw from any kind of relationship. Tidal waves of self-doubt and fear drive her to "safe" harbors of secrecy and defensiveness. She knows her friends are puzzled when she retreats, but she wants to avoid causing any more catastrophes in her life. She condemns herself for struggling with such "stupid feelings," then she feels ashamed of feeling ashamed. Memories of her family's accusations and her past sins mercilessly haunt her: "It's all true! I cannot deny what a failure I have been." She concludes that people are right to reject her, but her spirit recoils at the thought of their abandonment.

Shannon pleads with God for relief. But she knows it is impossible to undo her shameful past. And in spite of her best efforts, she is sure she disappoints the very people she wants to love. Again and again she fails. How can she ever truly be free?

Gwen

Gwen grew up in a stable, loving family. She went to church regularly and attended good schools. Today, Gwen is a manager with a reputable company, and she has a responsible husband and three healthy children. Life hasn't been easy, to be sure, but Gwen is generally happy and functioning well. Except for one thing. She feels like a failure. A person doesn't have to suffer abuse or rebellion to feel ashamed.

Like Shannon, Gwen has been sinned against, though in different ways. And she consistently falls short when she compares herself with her friends and coworkers. In spite of perpetual dieting, she is overweight. So she is always ashamed and self-conscious about her appearance. At work, Gwen feels incompetent when others tease her for making mistakes or jeer her when she follows company policies. She thinks, "If I were the parent I should be, my children wouldn't need so much correction!"

Gwen lives with a nebulous sense of spiritual shame, too. She knows she is a sinner saved by Christ's grace, but she feels the weight of her own inadequacies more than she does the love of her Savior. She asks for God's forgiveness almost constantly, but she doesn't feel forgiven.

Gwen tries to make up for her inadequacies through her many acts of service at home and in the community. But she doesn't feel included. Gwen generally feels like a fake. Though she tries, she can't shake an underlying sense of personal failure, disapproval, and shame.

Where do people like Shannon and Gwen turn? How can they overcome their sense of shame? You may be surprised to hear that Jesus Christ holds the answers to the problem of shame, so we will consult Scripture to see what Gwen and Shannon have missed. But before we examine God's solutions, we will look at two kinds of shame and some common responses to each.

Shame-Filled Living

Shame is "a painful [guilty] feeling due to the consciousness of having done or experienced something disgraceful ... the feeling of being caught doing something bad or ... of being seen while sinning."[2] Dr. Edward Welch describes shame-consciousness as "being exposed, vulnerable, and in desperate need of covering or protection. Under the gaze of the holy God and other people."[3]

Shame may follow sinful actions, or it may arise from accepting blame or failure. Whether guilt is real or imagined, shame holds a person hostage with

2 Johannes P. Louw and Eugene Albert Nida, *Greek–English Lexicon of the New Testament: Based on Semantic Domains* (electronic 2nd edn.; New York: United Bible Societies, 1996), 1:309.
3 Edward T. Welch, *When People Are Big and God Is Small: Overcoming Peer Pressure, Codependency, and the Fear of Man* (Phillipsburg, NJ: P&R, 1997), 24.

the condemning declaration, "You are bad!" Shannon and Gwen both live under that sentence. Perhaps you do, too.

No one likes feeling ashamed, but efforts to relieve shame often lead to frustration and increased distress. Below are some common reactions to persistent shame.

- ◗ Questioning God's goodness and/or sovereignty
- ◗ Doubting God's existence, love, and/or acceptance
- ◗ Rejecting God
- ◗ Social discomfort, leading to withdrawal
- ◗ Varying degrees of self-pity
- ◗ Mental and/or physical self-deprecation
- ◗ Self-sabotage or self-injury
- ◗ Addictive behaviors
- ◗ Wallowing in despair and self-doubt
- ◗ Indulging vengeful thoughts/actions, anger, and bitterness
- ◗ General irritability
- ◗ Anxiety and worry
- ◗ Perfectionism and/or legalism

▸ Escape or pursuit of relief through such means
  as daydreaming, overeating, overworking in
  career or ministry, intense pleasure-seeking,
  excessive socializing or social withdrawal,
  shopping, leaving home, adultery, divorce,
  or suicide

Perhaps you recognize some of these patterns in
yourself or a loved one. Some of them may seem
mild. But the results can be devastating to your soul
and your relationships, even with people who are far
removed from the source of your shame.

Shame generally takes two forms.

▸ "I am bad because of what I have done." In this
  case, personal sin produces guilt, and out of
  guilt may come feelings that we will call "sin-
  shame."

▸ "I am bad because of what other people have
  done." The sins of other people hurt you in
  ways that may cause feelings that we will
  call "provoked-shame."

Edward Welch describes these two sources of
shame: "Sin-shame is something we bring on
ourselves; [provoked-]shame is done to us. Everyone

13

has the experience of sin-shame, but not everyone has this shame intensified by [provoked-]shame."[4]

Sin-Shame

Sin-shame is the consequence of your actual guilt. When you offend God, the shame that results is true and right. If you have been mercilessly victimized, this may be hard news to hear. But it is important, so please read through this entire section. Liberating good news will follow.

SIN-SHAME IS A UNIVERSAL EXPERIENCE

Every person on earth, without exception, has committed what God calls *sin*. Sin is any thought or action that opposes or contradicts God.

One sin is all it takes to be a sinner.

> For whoever shall keep the whole law, and
> yet stumble in one point, he is guilty of all.
>
> (James 2:10)

---

4 Ibid., 26. Dr. Welch uses the term "victimization-shame" to describe the second type of shame that we will call "provoked-shame." I have substituted the word "provoked" to avoid confusion.

If you have ever lied, entertained a lustful thought, or used God's name flippantly, you are guilty because of what you have done. God clearly says there are no exceptions:

All have sinned.

(Romans 3:23)

Gwen is guilty of harboring grudges, complaining, overeating, disciplining her children in anger, and hating the body God created for her. When Shannon curses her uncle, refuses to forgive her mother, doubts God, cherishes bitterness, or mistreats her body, she sins. Both are responsible for their responses.

Sinful responses may seem understandable or even reasonable, and you may think you can make up for them later. But sin is serious:

For the wages of sin is death ...

(Romans 6:23)

Good deeds, penance, and self-reformation are insufficient to undo the effects or penalty of sin. Scripture declares,

We are all like an unclean thing,

15

> And all our righteousnesses [our best
> efforts] are like filthy rags.
>
> (Isaiah 64:6)

As hard as it is to hear this, sin-shame tells you the truth: "I am bad because of what I have done." Your guilt is real and irreversible. It needs to be addressed, but you are helpless to address it because you can't undo it. Therefore, you need God to forgive your sins, exchange your guilt for his righteousness (putting you into a right standing with God, based on the merits of Christ—2 Corinthians 5:21), and provide new life and identity that powerfully fight shame (Ephesians 1:3–6).

Sin-shame is actually merciful because it was designed to drive you to God for his free pardon in Jesus Christ. When you respond by repenting, sin-shame is no longer necessary, so God removes it. We will discuss this further in the next chapter. But first we will consider the second source of shame.

Provoked-Shame

From a young age Shannon experienced provoked-shame: "I am bad because of what others have done." Shannon's uncle and mother sinned in ways that hurt

Shannon and fostered her sense of self-condemnation and disgrace. Even today she feels betrayed, exposed, embarrassed, and confused. Ashamed.

As with sin-shame, provoked-shame condemns Shannon as a bad person. But unlike sin-shame, provoked-shame is a lie. No matter how she may feel, the sins of other people do not condemn Shannon in God's sight (Ezekiel 18:20). Provoked-shame condemns no one before God. But, if believed, its lies can do terrible damage.

Gwen's coworkers ridicule her. Her husband is highly critical. She falls short of society's definition of beauty. Her close friend betrays her confidence. Gwen accepts provoked-shame's lies and condemns herself based upon the words and actions of others. So Gwen feels helpless, embarrassed, disrespected, and frustrated. Ashamed.

Provoked-shame seems hopeless because the sufferer cannot prevent or fix the sins of others. As with sin-shame, someone outside the situation must intervene. Jesus Christ is that someone. But before we look at Christ's solutions for shame, we need to unpack the problem a bit more.

Mistaken Tendencies with Sin-Shame and Provoked-Shame

We have seen that sin-shame tells the truth: "I am bad because of what I have done." Sin-shame warns you of the condemnation of sin. When you heed the warning, sin-shame drives you to God. Therefore, sin-shame should be believed.

But provoked-shame lies to you—"I am bad because of what others have done"—and cruelly condemns you for something you can't control. Provoked-shame should be rejected.

The power of shame is broken when truth is believed and lies are rejected, as we shall see in the next few chapters. However, the common tendency is to reject the truth of sin-shame and accept the lies of provoked-shame.

WHEN YOU REJECT THE TRUTH OF SIN-SHAME

Generally, you can react to sin-shame in one of two ways: by believing you are guilty and accepting God's invitation to be forgiven in Christ, or by rejecting the truth of sin-shame and trying to deal with guilt on your own by excusing or denying sin, blame-shifting, or loathing yourself.

▶ Excusing or denying sin sounds like this: "What I did wasn't so bad. It wasn't really sin. I was just reacting normally. God understands how hard life is and won't hold this against me." But Scripture says every sin violates the purity and holiness of God; therefore, every sin offends him. Even one bite from forbidden fruit is enough to condemn you (Genesis 3). Christ had to die for even your smallest sins; they are that serious. "There is none righteous, no, not one" (Romans 3:10).

▶ Blame-shifting says, in effect, "My sin is understandable and acceptable because I was provoked. Someone else made me sin, so it's not my fault." But that attitude is not approved in Scripture. You are responsible for your responses to any situation. No one can make you sin; it is your choice. Christ is your example. Though he was brutally provoked, he did not sin. He provides all you need for godliness, so you have no excuse (Hebrews 4:14; 1 Peter 2:21–24; 2 Peter 1:3–9).

▶ Self-loathing goes to the other extreme. Instead of turning to God, the shame-driven person says, "I am so bad that I hate myself and must be punished. I must pay for my sins. Even Christ can't help me." But God asks you to come to him for forgiveness, not to punish yourself. Amy Baker writes, "When we sin against God, there should be some loathing. But that should lead us to repent, not wallow ... We are all bad. That's why we need a Savior. It is pride to believe I'm so bad I don't deserve to be forgiven when God has promised to forgive the worst of sinners."[5]

WHEN YOU ACCEPT THE LIES OF PROVOKED-SHAME

There are many ways to interpret and exercise provoked-shame. All of them involve accepting responsibility for what others do, rather than rejecting condemnation. Here are a few examples. More will follow in Chapter 4.

▶ "People criticize, hurt, and reject me; therefore, I must be bad." The truth: God does not and will not hold you responsible for the sins of others. Their criticisms, harmful actions, and rejection reflect on them, not on you (Romans 12:17–21; Proverbs 17:15).

5 Amy Baker, *Cutting: Bleeding the Pain Away* (FBCM: The Biblical Counselor's Toolbox Series; Lafayette, IN: Faith Resources, 2006), 17.

▶ "I fail to measure up/win approval/achieve, so I am bad." The truth: Human limitations do not condemn you in God's sight. "He remembers that we are dust ... The mercy of the LORD is from everlasting to everlasting" (Psalm 103:14, 17).

▶ "I suffer; therefore, I am at fault." God does not fault you for feeling pain or for suffering at the hands of oppressors. The sinless Christ himself suffered. He acknowledges the hardships you face, because he faced them, too (Hebrews 4:14–16). And he wants you to respond as he did.

CONSEQUENCES OF REJECTING TRUTH AND ACCEPTING LIES

It is not easy to discern between truth and lies, especially when you are suffering. Shannon is innocent of her uncle's sin, but her pain is real. His unspeakable actions have caused her to suffer, and he is accountable to God for what he has done. Though she is not responsible for his cruelties, she fails to see that her bitterness, fear, and rebellion are her contributions to the problem. Therefore, she does not address her sin-shame before God. Instead, she loathes herself and doubts God because of what her uncle did to her.

Gwen is ashamed of her appearance. Her sin-shame signals that she is responsible for the sins of ingratitude and gluttony, but she does not hear it. Instead, she fills her life with food and good works to try to silence her pain. She reads her Bible and goes to church, dons a happy face in public, and douses her soul with pleasant distractions. But she has withered inside because she has rejected her sin-shame. In addition, Gwen believes her husband's false accusations and internalizes her coworkers' jeering. She accepts the lie that she is at fault for their cruelties, and feels victimized by shame.

Have you recognized ways in which you contribute to your shame by accepting lies and rejecting truth? This is a difficult question, because it requires you to examine what you believe about God, yourself, and the people who have harmed you. Perhaps you don't want to unleash painful memories again. You may think that questioning a loved one constitutes disrespect or even unbelief. Or maybe you're afraid of further rejection. But I encourage you, dear reader, to move ahead now in a positive pursuit of truth about your shame. The truth, Christ has promised, will set you free.

Overcoming Shame

So far, we have identified two sources of shame and condemnation: your sin (sin-shame) and the sins of others (provoked-shame). Now we turn to the good news: Jesus Christ removes sin's condemnation (Romans 8:1) and despises (defies) shame.[6]

Jesus Christ Removes Sin's Condemnation

Biblical counselor Timothy Lane writes, "We experience shame because of our real guilt. Under-

---

6 Scripture is our navigator as we explore the solutions to shame. The Word of God supplies all we need for life and godliness, and reveals Jesus Christ as the truth (i.e., he doesn't just know the truth, but actually embodies it; John 1:1, 14; 14:6; 2 Peter 1:3. See also Psalm 19:7–14 and 2 Timothy 3:16–17). Therefore, your life will be transformed when you read Scripture to get to know Jesus Christ and follow him.

neath our anxiety, bitterness, and defensiveness is guilt. That is why we live with the feeling that we are not quite making the grade. We can't get rid of our shame until we address the problem of our real guilt."[7] Jesus Christ alone counteracts guilt, through grace alone by faith alone. Let's look more closely at this good news.

IN LOVE, GOD ANSWERS SIN-SHAME

> *For God so loved the world that He gave His only begotten Son, that whoever believes in Him should not perish but have everlasting life. For God did not send His Son into the world to condemn the world, but that the world through Him might be saved.*
>
> (John 3:16–17)

God opened the door to freedom when Jesus Christ took the sentence of death upon himself. He can offer forgiveness for sin because he lived a perfect life, fulfilling the requirements of God's Law that we have broken, and willingly offered that life as an atoning sacrifice on the cross. Our sin-shame is silenced by

7 Timothy S. Lane, *Freedom from Guilt: Finding Release from Your Burdens* (Greensboro, NC: New Growth Press, 2008), 15.

his righteousness, which is given to us when we put our faith in him.

GOD WON'T FORCE ANYONE TO ACCEPT HIS FORGIVENESS OF SIN

The gift of eternal life is free through Jesus Christ our Lord, but it is not yours until you receive it (Romans 6:23). No one automatically becomes a child of God.

> But as many as received Him, to them He gave the right to become children of God, to those who believe in His name.
>
> (John 1:12)

SCRIPTURE REVEALS HOW TO RECEIVE CHRIST

> If you confess with your mouth the Lord Jesus and believe in your heart that God has raised Him from the dead, you will be saved. For with the heart one believes unto righteousness, and with the mouth confession is made unto salvation. For the Scripture says, "Whoever believes on Him will not be put to shame."
>
> (Romans 10:9–11)

The forgiveness of Jesus Christ covers those who receive him by faith, no matter what sin has been committed or what atrocities have been experienced in this fallen world.

You Must Humble Yourself

You can only receive forgiveness by humbly admitting your sin and confessing your need for Christ's sacrifice. Approaching Christ with such an attitude is the necessary first step. He removes your sin-shame in forgiveness when you believe.

Did you notice the promise in Romans 10:11 above that "whoever believes on Him will not be put to shame"? Here is God's magnificent promise that in Christ the full payment for your sin has been made forever. "There is therefore now no condemnation to those who are in Christ Jesus" (Romans 8:1a). No one who receives Christ by faith will ever be rejected by God.

Take a moment to examine yourself. Was there ever a time when you humbled yourself before God, confessed your sin, and trusted him alone to forgive you? No penance, no self-improvement projects—just belief in the death, burial, and resurrection of Jesus Christ as payment for your sin (1 Corinthians 15:1–4).

When you humbly come to Christ for salvation,

God makes unconditional promises to remove condemnation and adopt you into his family forever, thereby assuring you of a secure relationship with him (John 5:24; Romans 8:1, 14–17) and a home in heaven after death (2 Corinthians 5:1). Those blessings will never be removed.

The Continuing Battle with Feelings of Shame

You may recall that Gwen and Shannon both received Christ as children. After years of rebellion, Shannon turned back to Christ. Gwen never overtly turned away. Yet the two women continue to wrestle with shame. Why?

SIN-SHAME CONTINUES TO TELL YOU THE TRUTH AND DRIVE YOU TO GOD

One reason why feelings of shame continue is that sin continues. Until you reach heaven, you will struggle with this fallen world, the devil, and your own sinful habits (Romans 7). Though condemnation is gone, you still have to fight against sin (Ephesians 6:11–13). The good news is that in Christ you have the power to overcome sin and grow in his likeness.

27

> For sin shall not have dominion over you,
> for you are not under law but under grace.
> (Romans 6:14)

God continues to use your sin-shame to drive you to Christ, where you are to humble yourself and admit where you need to change. This is the essence of Christian growth, and victory is assured when you submit in obedience to the process. But pride resists humility. In an article about Peter's refusal to allow Jesus to wash his feet, Winston Smith describes the battle:

> *At least part of us would find prideful satisfaction in being able to take care of our own mess. But another sizeable part would like to avoid having another, especially Jesus, see our filth. And the thought of Jesus having to touch it ... well, that makes us just want to say no ... Jesus' message is as direct and startling as Peter's. "Unless I wash you, you have no part of me" (John 13:8). Well, that clinches it, doesn't it? Jesus insists on putting an end to both our pride and our shame ...*
>
> *We must acknowledge just how faulted we*

*have become. We trod through a fallen
world. We tramp through the mess of
our own sin and we've been smeared
by the sinful deeds of others. We are
rebellious. We are wounded. We are
proud. We are ashamed. We need all of
it washed away ... Whether it's shame or
pride, part of me doesn't want Jesus to
cleanse me. But there's no other way.*[8]

God uses sin-shame to signal that your old sinful habits of thought and behavior need to be replaced with new Scripture-driven ones. But you can focus on your faults and sins so much that you deny the completeness of forgiveness and righteousness in Christ. Shameful thoughts feed on emotion, reason, and experience, not Scripture. When you dwell in shame, your feelings declare, "It doesn't matter what the Bible says. I believe my shame." In that mindset, you may neglect or misuse Scripture to focus on condemnation rather than to look worshipfully at Christ. Self-deprecation, negativism, anger, fear, and anxiety live where

8 Winston Smith, "Do You Want to Say 'No' to Jesus' Touch?",
   in *Vital Signs* (newsletter of the Christian Counseling
   Education Foundation), Fall 2010.

Scripture's true meaning has no toehold.

Responding Biblically

CHANGE YOUR DESIRES

Though truth is unchanging, God allows you to choose what you will believe and live for. Those choices are based upon what you want most. Therefore, it is important to evaluate what you desire.

You probably desire good things. Like Shannon and Gwen, you want people to love you. Being loved is good. When you feel loved, you thrive. But when rejected, you may feel like retaliating, wallowing, or isolating yourself.

Your reactions to rejection reveal your true desires. God wants you to respond with love for him first and then for your neighbor (Matthew 22:37–39). Christ demonstrated love when his enemies rejected him. Is that your usual response? If not, your desires need to change.

Shannon is not satisfied with being accepted in Christ (Ephesians 1:6). She wants certain people to accept her too—people of her choice. She is willing to rebel, wallow, and complain if she doesn't get what she wants. Shannon's sin-shame warns her that she should evaluate her motives. When she is willing to sin, her desire for acceptance is more important to her than following Christ's example.

Where sin-shame reveals your sinful desires, thoughts, and actions, you are responsible for making changes. You should take that responsibility seriously.

THINK BIBLICALLY

Shame is self-condemning. But 1 John 1:9 declares,

> If we confess our sins, He [God] is faithful
> and just to forgive us our sins and to cleanse
> us from all unrighteousness.

Confession means wholeheartedly agreeing with God about your sins as you turn to obey Christ.

God's cleansing is complete and does not depend on your feelings or the depths of your sin.

▶ You should confess your sins no matter how you feel.

▶ First John 1:9 does not require a complete listing of every sin that you have committed (no one's memory is that good!). But you should confess the specific sins that God has brought to your mind.

31

▶ Scripture promises that God forgives and cleanses all your sins when you confess. Choose to believe God's Word on that, even if you don't feel forgiven. Trust Scripture (not your feelings) to tell you the truth.

▶ Humbly agree with God that your sin is ugly and despicable, and plan to change your thoughts and actions to line up with Scripture.

▶ Stop beating yourself up. Instead, accept forgiveness in Christ. Tell yourself the truth: "And you, being dead in your trespasses ..., He has made alive together with Him, having forgiven you all trespasses, having wiped out the handwriting of requirements that was against us, which was contrary to us. And He has taken it out of the way, having nailed it to the cross" (Colossians 2:13–14).

▶ Remind yourself that you stand righteous before God by faith in Christ (Philippians 3:9). Your position in him is not maintained by good works, but by Christ's payment for your sins. Therefore, you can never lose it (Ephesians 2:8–9).

After you confess your sins, anchor yourself in the fact that Christ has completely forgiven and cleansed you.

ACT BIBLICALLY

Follow the example of Christ, who leads and transforms believers. To follow Christ means wholeheartedly seeking to know and please God in thought, motivation, and behavior. You may think you cannot please God because of your faults and failures. But because you are forgiven in Christ, God is pleased with your sincere effort to follow Scripture. Reject doubts about his goodness, forgiveness, or love (2 Corinthians 3:18; 7:9–11; Romans 8:29; James 1:6–8). That is the way, day by day, to grow into his likeness. Shame cannot dwell in that environment. Edward Welch writes,

> *Call out to the Lord, don't cry on your bed. Face your doubts about God's plans for your life. Right now it feels like misery, but if God sent Jesus to die so we could live, why would he be uncaring now? God's plans include hardship and disappointment, but his love has already been proven in Jesus, and it is more sophisticated than we know. Even in our hardship he is doing good. Sometimes the good is teaching us to trust him. It is a spiritual response with eternal value.*[9]

9 Edward T. Welch, *Self-Injury: When Pain Feels Good* (Phillipsburg, NJ: P&R, 2004), 23.

33

Sin-shame is appropriately addressed by receiving Christ's forgiveness and following his example as Scripture requires. Next we will look at how Christ and our new identity in him defuse provoked-shame.

Embracing Your New Identity in Christ

Second Corinthians 4:2 calls you to renounce shame: "But we have renounced the hidden things of shame, not walking in craftiness nor handling the word of God deceitfully, but by manifestation of the truth commending ourselves to every man's conscience in the sight of God" (2 Corinthians 4:2). To renounce means "to refuse to follow, obey, or recognize any further."[10]

Renounce Provoked-Shame with Humility, As Christ Did

Christ's example provides hope because he refused to follow or even acknowledge provoked-shame, even while he was mocked, beaten, and hung naked

10 "Renounce," *Merriam-Webster's Collegiate Dictionary* (10th edn.; Springfield, MA: Merriam-Webster, 1999), 991.

to die on a cross. He "endured the cross, despising the shame" (Hebrews 12:2b) by defying shame and directing his thoughts against it. This response may not seem like humility to you, but it was. Rather than allowing shame to infiltrate his thoughts as his accusers mocked him, and rather than submitting to anger and fear as he was abused, he humbly accepted what God had given him to do. Though he was the eternal Son of God, "He humbled Himself and became obedient to the point of death, even the death of the cross" (Philippians 2:8b).

Christ Despised Shame

Christ was despised and rejected by men (Isaiah 53:3). Yet in return he chose not to despise people, but, rather, to despise the shame they tried to inflict on him.

> Therefore we also, since we are surrounded
> by so great a cloud of witnesses, let us
> lay aside every weight, and the sin which
> so easily ensnares us, and let us run with
> endurance the race that is set before us,
> looking unto Jesus, the author and finisher
> of our faith, who for the joy that was set
> before Him endured the cross, despising the

> shame, and has sat down at the right hand
> of the throne of God. For consider Him
> who endured such hostility from sinners
> against Himself, lest you become weary and
> discouraged in your souls.
>
> (Hebrews 12:1–3)

How easily our Savior could have raged or fallen into despair at the abandonment, abuse, humiliation, and injustice he experienced! He would have been completely justified. But rather than dwelling on the wrongs done to him, Christ rejected shame by remembering his identity, embracing the purposes of his Father, focusing on his part in God's plan, and looking forward to the joy ahead of him.

CHRIST EMBRACED HIS IDENTITY

Christ rejected rejection. Instead, he accepted his identity as defined by his Father (Philippians 2:9–11).

New life in Christ brings new identity to you, too. As a child of God, you are defined as eternally beloved, chosen, holy, adopted, forgiven, and redeemed in Christ (see Ephesians 1:3–8). No one can take that away. You are accepted in the beloved one (Jesus Christ), no matter what anyone else says (Ephesians 1:6). Rather than "looking at [yourself]

37

and [your] sense of unworthiness and filthiness, rather than trying to hide from God, believe the words of Christ. You are not beyond God's grace."[11] Humble and deliberate acceptance of your true identity in God's family declaws shame for you, just as it did for Christ.

CHRIST EMBRACED THE PURPOSES OF HIS FATHER

God had an eternal purpose for Christ's suffering: to provide the way of redemption for mankind. So, too, the trials in your life hold eternal value in God's hands. He has given you something to do. Lay aside your starving dreams and embrace his plan for you.

> In Him also we have obtained an
> inheritance, being predestined according
> to the purpose of Him who works all things
> according to the counsel of His will.
>
> (Ephesians 1:11)

> But we have this treasure in earthen vessels,
> that the excellence of the power may be of
> God and not of us. We are hard-pressed on
> every side, yet not crushed; we are perplexed,

---

11 Welch, *When People Are Big and God Is Small*, 67.

> but not in despair; persecuted, but not
> forsaken; struck down, but not destroyed ...
> *We do not look at the things which are seen,*
> *but at the things which are not seen. For the*
> *things which are seen are temporary, but the*
> *things which are not seen are eternal.*
>
> (2 Corinthians 4:7–9, 18)

CHRIST FOCUSED ON HIS ROLE IN GOD'S PLAN

Christ's role was to die to take away the sins of the world. A difficult position, to be sure, but an essential one.

Where would you be right now if Christ had not fulfilled his role by dying in your place and rising from the dead? Imagine if he had listened to provoked-shame instead. He would have resented you instead of loving you. He would have believed himself to be a failure because people rejected him, wallowed in his physical helplessness and pain, and lost his perspective. Instead of providing redemption, he would have brought vengeance upon those whom he had been called to save. Eternal life would have been lost to you. The human race would completely perish in sin!

But Christ loved his Father and he loved you. Therefore, he despised shame and willingly died, knowing that he was accomplishing God's will. You are required to do the same. Jesus said,

> If anyone desires to come after Me, let him
> deny himself, and take up his cross daily,
> and follow Me. For whoever desires to save
> his life will lose it, but whoever loses his life
> for My sake will save it.
>
> (Luke 9:23–24)

Put effort into denying your demand for human acceptance and freedom from pain. Instead, choose to follow God's highest commandments to love God and other people wholeheartedly, as Christ did (Matthew 22:37–39). He actively chose to die to save sinners. Through him, death is overcome, and you are now called to live to share the gospel and make disciples for his sake, not to be defined and overcome by shame (Matthew 28:19–20; 2 Corinthians 5:15).[12] When you live for Christ, your focus is drawn away from the hardships in this world, and a sense of purpose is born. Choose to believe that God has

---

12 If you are currently in an abusive situation, you should seek
   help both physically and spiritually. For assistance, consult
   the booklet *Help! Someone I Love Has Been Abused* by
   Jim Newheiser, also in the Living in a Fallen World series
   (Leominster: Day One, 2010).

equipped you for the good work he created you to do (Ephesians 2:8–10). In a sound biblical church, learn how you can get busy serving him.

CHRIST LOOKED AHEAD TO THE JOY BEFORE HIM

He had an eternal perspective. Christ did his work to rescue souls as he looked forward to returning to heaven. Choose that kind of focus. Partake joyfully in bringing other souls to Jesus. Be confident that your trials are temporary and have a valuable purpose. And look forward, as did Christ, to your glorious home in heaven.

Choose Humility as a Means to Despise Shame

Provoked-shame could not condemn Christ because he chose to humble himself before his Father. In so doing, he despised the shame. You can overcome shame the same way.

But how? Aren't humility and shame the same thing? When you tell yourself how flawed you are or when you mentally replay your failures, aren't you being humble?

In a word, no. Shame and humility are vastly different. Stuart Scott defines humility as "The

41

mindset of Christ (a servant's mindset): a focus on God and others, a pursuit of the recognition and the exaltation of God, and a desire to glorify and please God in all things and by all things He has given."[13] Whereas humility is based upon God's grace, shame denies grace and perpetuates misery.

The chart opposite illustrates how exercising humility simultaneously despises shame because the two are mutually exclusive. You cannot be humble and full of shame at the same time. To choose one is to exclude the other.

CHOOSE CHRIST'S HUMBLE ATTITUDE

Christlike humility submits single-heartedly to God's agenda, because of the wise, just, and loving nature of God. Christ disregarded his own reputation in favor of his role in the salvation of mankind because he knew God's plan was best. His service included unspeakable suffering, humiliation, and pain. But believing in the good purposes of his Father, Christ glorified God in his suffering.

Shannon and Gwen's hearts focus on another agenda. Though they hate how they feel, they follow their provoked-shame. How about you? Are

13 Stuart Scott, *From Pride to Humility: A Biblical Perspective* (rev. edn.; Bemidji, MN: Focus, 2002), 17–18.

PRINCIPLE	HUMILITY	SHAME
Perception of God	Believes God's character is good	Believes God is distant and uncaring, or harsh and punitive
Meaning in life	Focuses biblically and submits to God's purposes; pursues meaningful direction	Focuses on and submits to self-condemnation; feels meaningless
Motivation and source of truth	Hears and embraces God's Word	Hears negativity and dwells on hardship
Example	Follows Christ's example	Follows fear and doubt
Theology of suffering	Recognizes the value of suffering in God's will	Doubts God for allowing suffering
Responses to persecution	Endures by faith and counts it joy	Weeps without hope and seeks escape
Attitude	Gives thanks in hard times	Negative thinking; wallows
Liberty	Free in Christ	Imprisoned in self
Self-image	Sees worth in Christ	Sees self as worthless but craves self-worth
Focus	Focuses on Christ and the gospel	Focuses on fear and injustice
Desires	Craves God's honor	Craves something for self
Fear	Fears God and stands in awe of him	Fears man's actions and opinions; fears the future
Love	Understands God's love is freely given, based on Christ's sacrifice and God's character	Thinks God's love is unattainable, based on human character

other people's actions and opinions more powerful over you than God? Humble yourself, deny lies and destructive reactions, and follow Christ instead.

CHOOSE CHRIST'S HUMBLE THINKING

> Let this mind be in you which was also in Christ Jesus, who, being in the form of God, did not consider it robbery to be equal with God, but made Himself of no reputation, taking the form of a bondservant, and coming in the likeness of men.
>
> (Philippians 2:5–7)

Following Christ's agenda means denying your natural tendencies and replacing unbiblical thoughts with the mind of Christ (Ephesians 4:22–32).

Shannon's provoked-shame is perpetuated by negative thoughts about herself: her failures, her family's offenses, and her hopelessness. Instead, she should choose to humbly focus on Christ, by whose grace we are made free.

> Humble yourselves in the sight of the Lord, and He will lift you up.
>
> (James 4:10)

> [Be] confident of this very thing, that He
> who has begun a good work in you will
> complete it until the day of Jesus Christ.
>
> *(Philippians 1:6)*

Gwen tells herself, "Because people treat me poorly, I'll never amount to anything. I'm a failure." But she can turn her mind to Scripture that says,

> I can do all things through Christ who
> strengthens me.
>
> *(Philippians 4:13)*

> You are complete in Him, who is the head
> of all principality and power.
>
> *(Colossians 2:10)*

Both women have built their lives upon a false foundation. Perhaps your beliefs, like theirs, also contradict Scripture. To follow Christ, humble yourself by admitting that you have accepted lies. Scripture says,

> We have renounced the hidden things
> of shame.
>
> *(2 Corinthians 4:2)*

45

> Let us lay aside every weight, and the sin
> which so easily ensnares us, and let us
> run with endurance the race that is set
> before us.
>
> (Hebrews 12:1)

FOLLOW CHRIST'S HUMBLE ACTIONS

The beauty of Christ's humility is seen in the demonstration of his love toward the very people who treated him poorly.

- He forgave them. Consider his patience toward his disciples, who misunderstood him, failed to support him, and ran away in his hour of need. He did not treat them as their sin deserved. He treated them according to his Father's love for his creatures. He has done the same for you, and he calls you to follow his example.

- He served them. His life on earth was a picture of selfless service and grace toward his enemies. He actively sought their well-being rather than getting back at them (see Romans 12:14; Colossians 1:21).

- He spoke truth in love to them. Christ acted justly, but he never complained or sought vengeance when he was treated unjustly. His statements on the cross were all directed at ministry to others and submission to the Father. He left the results to God, and he asks you to do the same (Romans 12:17–21).[14]

▶ He considered others before himself. His name is "above every name," and he is the one to whom "every knee should bow, of those in heaven, and of those on earth, and of those under the earth" (Philippians 2:9–10). But he willingly laid all that glory aside for your sake (Matthew 20:28).

---

14 Justice may also involve biblical confrontation, church and/or governmental intervention, and other consequences that go beyond the scope of this booklet. See your pastor or a biblical counselor for help.

Renouncing All Shame in Christ

Following Christ includes honoring him in your responses to the events and people in your life, even when they are evil and harmful. While Christ never excused his oppressors, he also did not demand to be honored, loved, revered, or considered. Instead, he stood for truth and lived for his Father's purposes. His humility is our model for overcoming shame, even when bad memories and some consequences may still remain.[15] Let's look more closely at how that is accomplished.

Gwen's Temptation

Gwen humbles herself before God and commits her life to him afresh. But later that day her husband

15 Christ's scars remain (John 20:27).

falsely accuses her of failing to discipline their children. Provoked-shame arises and she feels hurt. Out of habit she thinks, "I'll never be a good mom. My kids don't stand a chance with such a bad mother."

GWEN RENOUNCES SHAME

▶ *Humble attitude.* Feelings of shame interrupt Gwen's thoughts. She regards the alert and prays for wisdom. She realizes that Christ wants her to humble herself and stop her negative thinking. (Notice that she does not deny that her husband has sinned, nor does she accept responsibility for his role in the wrongdoing. But she chooses an attitude of grace rather than resentment.)

▶ *Biblical thinking.* Gwen considers how she could improve her parenting skills and communicate to her husband in a way that honors Christ. She thinks about how to overcome evil with good.

▶ *Biblical action.* Gwen follows through wisely by seeking her husband's advice. She treats him respectfully, even when he continues to be critical and harsh, because that is what Christ did when people were critical and harsh with him. In other words, she reacts according to Christ's example rather than her husband's. In

49

addition, she asks a godly woman how she can be a more biblical parent.

Shannon's Temptation

Shannon has a lot of bad memories to overcome, especially when her uncle's sins come to mind.

SHANNON RENOUNCES SHAME

▶ *Humble attitude.* Shannon's resentment against her uncle causes sin-shame, which reminds her that she too is a sinner. She decides to overcome anger and shame with biblical forgiveness.[16]

▶ *Biblical thinking.* Shannon chooses to dwell on the fact that her sin sent Christ to the cross, yet he responded graciously by offering her forgiveness and new life (Romans 5:8). Shannon does not excuse her uncle's sin, but she puts away her anger by being "kind ..., tenderhearted, forgiving ..., even as God in

16 We are unable to offer a thorough discussion of forgiveness in this booklet. But the subject is very important. We recommend the booklet *Forgive! As Christ Has Forgiven You* by Patrick Morison (Phillipsburg, NJ: P&R, 1997) and the book *When Forgiveness Doesn't Make Sense* by Robert Jeffress (Colorado Springs, CO: Waterbrook Press, 2000).

Christ forgave [her]" (Ephesians 4:32).

▶ *Biblical action.* In following through on
forgiving her uncle as Christ has forgiven her,
Shannon takes action by promising not to
hold his sin against him anymore. Instead, she
remembers that God promises to bring justice
(Romans 12:17–21). Because she has carried
resentment for many years, she must renew her
promise of forgiveness often because it comes
up frequently in her mind. Thus she honors
God. Whenever shame creeps in, she reminds
herself that God is pleased with her growth
even though she still has a long way to go
(Galatians 6:8–10; James 1:22–25).

Gwen's Temptation

Because she is overweight, Gwen despises her
appearance.

Gwen Renounces Shame

▶ *Humble attitude.* Gwen admits that she has
been insulting the One who created her
body (Psalm 139:13–18) and has been fearing
rejection rather than loving God and other

people (Matthew 22:37–39). Thus sin-shame is part of the problem. When she catches herself making comparisons, Gwen confesses her sinful thinking and accepts the full forgiveness of God.

▶ *Biblical thinking.* Rather than wallowing in displeasure, Gwen decides to compare her shame-laden thoughts with Scripture. She sees that she fuels her own shame when she unfavorably compares herself with her peers. Scripture says that "[others], measuring themselves by themselves, and comparing themselves among themselves, are not wise" (2 Corinthians 10:12).

▶ *Biblical action.* Gwen realizes she has accepted the world's standard of beauty. Instead, she gives thanks for how God has fashioned her body and her life (1 Thessalonians 5:18). In addition, she seeks to become a better steward of her body by eating and exercising wisely, then choosing to be content with how she looks (1 Timothy 4:8; Philippians 4:12). Thus, she repents of sin-shame, despises provoked-shame, and brings glory to God (1 Corinthians 10:31).

Gwen and Shannon learn to treat their feelings of shame as a signal to biblically examine their thoughts, motives, and actions. The chart on the following pages demonstrates more ways to renounce shame by thinking and acting biblically. I have provided just a few examples here. Spend time in God's Word to learn more about overcoming shame God's way. The passages in the chart will help you get started in your new way of life.

Change takes much diligent effort, consistency, and patient endurance. But keep at it. Get involved in a gospel-driven, biblical local church where you can learn more about God's purposes and your roles.

Growth into Christlikeness is a lifelong process. Through Christ's forgiveness and example of humility, shame can be progressively overcome. You can refuse to dwell in the dark secret world of shame any longer if you choose to confess sin-shame and renounce provoked-shame whenever you recognize them. Every time you respond biblically, you please and honor God (Romans 12:21).

Renouncing Shame

Shame-Driven Thoughts and Behaviors	Biblical Humility (H), Thinking (T), and Action (A)
Love and Merit Shannon: "No one loves me. But they should." Gwen: "I'll never be good enough to merit love from anyone, but I'm angry at being put into this position."	(H) Love is a gift, not a right. It can't be earned, manipulated, or demanded. God loves me deeply because he is good, not because I deserve to be loved (John 3:16; 1 John 4:7–19). (T) God's gift of love will never end (Romans 8:31–39; 1 Corinthians 13:8a). Because his love is complete, I have all I need in him (Colossians 2:9–10). (A) Self-pity, angry demands for love, or wallowing have no place in the life of a believer. Instead, God wants me to respond to his love by loving others the way he loves me (John 15:12; 1 Corinthians 13:1–8; 1 John 4:11).
Suffering Isn't Fair! Shannon: "Bad things happened to me; therefore I am bad, a slut, a liar, an idiot. But it isn't fair that there's no way out." Gwen: "It isn't fair because I am innocent and shouldn't have to change. Why did God make me like this?"	(H) Bad things happen to everyone because we live in a fallen world (Romans 8:22). I am not bad because of what has happened to me (see Hebrews 11, esp. vv. 37–38). I am bad because I sin against God by nature and by choice (Romans 3:10–12, 23). God didn't make me sin. That is my fault. It would be fair for God to condemn me. But, instead, God has provided forgiveness through the Savior, Jesus Christ (Romans 6:23). (T) God doesn't make me wallow; I choose what I dwell on. In Christ I have hope and a new identity, so I must not call myself names or doubt his purpose for my life (2 Corinthians 5:17–21). (A) I will think and act as Christ did when bad things happened to him (Philippians 4:13; 1 Peter 2:21–24).

Self-Image

Shannon: "People tell me I'm bad and stupid. I know I'm not perfect, so they must be right. I can't change; so I'll pretend or hide, even from God. He must not love me."

Gwen: "People don't treat me well, and I know I'm not perfect, so I must be at fault. I'm stupid, stupid, stupid! But I'll put on a happy face for everyone and pretend everything is OK."

(H) My fears of people's opinions deny God's power and love toward me (2 Timothy 1:7). Yes, I am imperfect, but Christ has forgiven me and is leading me to grow in grace (Colossians 1:10; 2:14).

(T) I must wisely choose to believe Scripture, no matter what people say (2 Corinthians 4:2). Even if I don't know why people think poorly of me, I must follow Christ. People thought poorly of him and treated him badly, but he was perfect. I am imperfect, but every day I can choose to be more like my Savior by responding to poor treatment the way he did. And that pleases him (2 Corinthians 5:9). I do right when I choose to follow Christ, no matter what people tell me. Ultimately I must put my hope in Christ, not in people (Romans 15:13).

Using Scripture, have I evaluated whether people think poorly of me because I have sinned against them? If so, I must confess my sins to God and the people I have offended (Matthew 5:23–24; 1 John 1:9–10). If not, I must forgive those who have offended me (Romans 12:17–21; Ephesians 4:31–32).

(A) My purpose is to shine for Christ even when life is hard, not to focus on my flaws or listen to unwise people (Matthew 5:16; Psalms 55–57). God has made me his beloved child (Ephesians 1:4–6) and he wants me to live boldly for him, not to hide (Philippians 1:19–20). To live for Christ means living for the truth, not pretending to be something I'm not (John 14:6).

Failure

Shannon and Gwen: "I'm not as good as other people. My appearance, education, intelligence, social skills, background, and family all fall short. I'll never be good enough. Look at what I've done! Look at how I fail. I try my best, but I mess up all the time. How could anyone accept a miserable person like me?"

(H) Christ had "no form or comeliness ... no beauty that we should desire Him," yet he was perfect (Isaiah 53:2). Inner beauty is what God values (1 Peter 3:3–6). Is that what I value most?

(T) In Christ I am accepted and dearly loved (Ephesians 1:4–6). Though even as a believer I still have faults, Christ does not hold them against me (2 Corinthians 5:19; Psalm 103:12) but teaches me to be like him (Hebrews 12:11). God has given me my appearance, education, intelligence, social skills, background, and family; I must give thanks to my Creator for them (1 Thessalonians 5:18).

(A) Therefore, I am responsible for loving others rather than comparing myself unfavorably with them (2 Corinthians 10:12).

Painful Memories

Shannon: "Bad memories persist, no matter what I do, and I feel badly about what has happened to me. Those events have made me what I am. Since I can't change my past, there is no hope."

Gwen: "See all the ways people have hurt me!"

(H) The Psalms teach me how to faithfully endure hardship without denying pain, but with gratitude for God's presence and help (Psalms 55–57, 73).

(T) I can acknowledge pain while recognizing that in Christ all things are made new (2 Corinthians 5:17), that God has good purposes for every event in my life (1 Peter 5:7–10), that Christ now defines me (Ephesians 1:3–21). I always have hope in Christ (Ephesians 1:18–19).

(A) Christ has bad memories, too, but he commits everything to his Father and focuses on God's purposes rather than his pain. I please God when I follow Christ's example (1 Peter 2:21–25).

CONCLUSION

Shame does not have to define you. In Christ you can have forgiveness, a new identity, and a new way to live—in his righteousness and humility. Respond to sin-shame by receiving Christ's forgiveness for your sin and then learning to live as he did. Renounce provoked-shame by choosing biblical humility and turning your thoughts and actions to follow Scripture.

If you consistently turn to truth and reject lies, looking to Christ and following his example as Scripture teaches, his grace will overshadow and defuse your shame.

Regular attendance at a sound biblical church will help you to grow in scriptural knowledge and faithful service. If you need additional help, a good biblical counselor can assist you further in your journey.

Personal Application Projects

1. Responding Biblically

Refuse to let your feelings tell you what to do. No matter how strongly you feel, inform your feelings with Scripture. Here are some steps you can take.

Every day, for two to three weeks, keep a journal.

▶ When you feel ashamed, try to identify what circumstances or people triggered those feelings. When you started to feel ashamed, what was happening? Who was involved? If you were alone, what thoughts were going through your mind?

▶ Record any reasons you felt/feel ashamed.

▶ To the best of your ability, identify if you are dealing with sin-shame, provoked-shame, or a combination. (See below.)

▶ Write how you responded to shame. What did you think? What did you do?

▶ Use the charts in this booklet to help you identify the lies you follow. Force yourself to turn your thoughts. In other words, replace each lie with Scripture (truth) every time you feel ashamed.

▶ Write down how you will act differently, according to the truth. At the end of each day, log how you followed through with those actions.

▶ Pray from verses such as Colossians 1:9–12, Philippians 2:5, and 2 Corinthians 10:5. Write the verses down and keep them at hand.

Continue this process whenever you feel ashamed.

2. More Help for Sin-Shame

The answer to sin-shame is to confess your sins and choose to believe that Christ has fully forgiven you. (Note: Scripture nowhere commands you to forgive yourself. Simply receive and believe Christ's forgiveness.)

▶ Name the specific sins that you need to confess.

▶ Read 1 John 1:8–2:2. Confessing sin means agreeing with God and turning away from that sin. In these verses, what does God say he will do if you confess your sins? How complete is his forgiveness?

▶ Write down some of the ways your wrong actions have caused trouble for you. Write your plan to stop your sin and do right instead.

▶ Write down your plan to fulfill any responsibilities you have been neglecting. Ask someone to help you be accountable for following through with your plan.

▶ Read 1 John 2:1–2 again. An "Advocate" comes to your defense. According to this passage, does Christ seek to punish or shame you? What is he doing instead?

▶ Ask for help from a biblical counselor if your feelings of shame don't improve.

3. More Help for Provoked-Shame

Read Proverbs 29:25. Using the examples below, write down how you will despise shame by showing Christlike love to other people instead of fearing what they think of you. (Note: Love means giving for the well-being of the other person, regardless of whether he or she deserves it, and regardless of how he or she responds.)

▎ Someone criticizes you. *How will you treat that person when you next see him or her?*

▎ You do poorly on a test. *What will you say to your classmate who does well?*

▎ Your boss frowns at you. *How will you respond to his or her frown?*

▎ You see some disapproving looks as you rush into church late. *What will you choose to think about during the service? How will you show love to your pastor? To those who disapproved of you?*

▎ You see someone from your past, and bad memories are triggered. *How will you greet that person?*

Read Romans 12:9–21. Using each verse, write out how to respond to people biblically.[17] What specific actions from these verses do you think God wants you to take next? Write that into your schedule this week. Journal the results. Then take the next step. Keep going, no matter how you feel.

17 Note: Forgiveness means you won't hold the offense against the offender anymore. Is there anyone you should forgive? Write his or her name down. Whom have you offended? Write how you will ask for that person's forgiveness. For important additional help with forgiveness, refer to the resources list or see a biblical counselor.

61

Where Can I Get Further Help?

To locate a biblical counselor in your area, visit www.nanc.org. If outside the USA, email info@nanc.org for resources and possible referrals.

Jeffress, Robert, *When Forgiveness Doesn't Make Sense* (Colorado Springs: Waterbrook Press, 2000)

Lane, Timothy, *Freedom from Guilt: Finding Release from Your Burdens* (Greensboro, NC: New Growth Press, 2008)

Morison, Patrick, *Forgive! As Christ Has Forgiven You* (Phillipsburg, NJ: P&R, 1997)

Scott, Stuart, *From Pride to Humility: A Biblical Perspective* (rev. edn.; Bemidji, MN: Focus, 2002)

Van Stone, Dorie, and Lutzer, Ernest, *Dorie: The Girl Nobody Loved* (Chicago: Moody Bible Institute, 1979)

Welch, Edward T., *Self-Injury: When Pain Feels Good* (Phillipsburg, NJ: P&R, 2004)

Welch, Edward T., *When People Are Big and God Is Small: Overcoming Peer Pressure, Codependency, and the Fear of Man* (Phillipsburg, NJ: P&R, 1997)

Booklets in the *Help!* series include ...

(More titles in preparation)